BIOGRAPHY FROM
ANCIENT CIVILIZATIONS
LEGENDS, FOLKLORE, AND STORIES OF ANCIENT WORLDS

The Life and Times of

ERIK THE RED

Mitchell Lane
PUBLISHERS

P.O. Box 196
Hockessin, Delaware 19707
www.mitchelllane.com

TITLES IN THE SERIES

BIOGRAPHY FROM ANCIENT CIVILIZATIONS

LEGENDS, FOLKLORE, AND STORIES OF ANCIENT WORLDS

The Life and Times of

ERIK THE RED

Earle Rice Jr.

Mitchell Lane PUBLISHERS

Printing   1   2   3   4   5   6   7   8   9

Library of Congress Cataloging-in-Publication Data
Rice, Earle.
  The life and times of Erik the Red / by Earle Rice, Jr.
    p. cm. — (Biography from ancient civilizations)
  Includes bibliographical references and index.
  ISBN 978-1-58415-701-4 (library bound)
  1. Eric, the Red, fl. 985—Juvenile literature. 2. Explorers—America—Biography—Juvenile literature. 3. Explorers—Norway—Biography—Juvenile literature. 4. Vikings—Biography—Juvenile literature. 5. America—Discovery and exploration—Norse—Juvenile literature. 6. Greenland—Discovery and exploration—Norse—Juvenile literature. 7. Vikings—Greenland—History—Juvenile literature. I. Title.
  E105.E67R53 2009
  910.92—dc22
  [B]
                                                                    2008020931

ABOUT THE AUTHOR: Earle Rice Jr. is a former senior design engineer and technical writer in the aerospace, electronic-defense, and nuclear industries. He has devoted full time to his writing since 1993 and is the author of more than fifty published books, including *A Brief Political and Geographic History of Latin America: Where Are Gran Colombia, La Plata, and Dutch Guiana?*, *Blitzkrieg! Hitler's Lightning War*, *The Life and Times of Leif Eriksson*, and *Canaletto* for Mitchell Lane Publishers. Earle is listed in *Who's Who in America* and is a member of the Society of Children's Book Writers and Illustrators, the League of World War I Aviation Historians, the Air Force Association, and the Disabled American Veterans.

PUBLISHER'S NOTE: This story is based on the author's extensive research, which he believes to be accurate. Documentation of such research is contained on page 46.

The internet sites referenced herein were active as of the publication date. Due to the fleeting nature of some web sites, we cannot guarantee they will all be active when you are reading this book.

To reflect current usage, we have chosen to use the secular era designations BCE ("before the common era") and CE ("of the common era") instead of the traditional designations BC ("before Christ") and AD (*anno Domini*, "in the year of the Lord").

PHOTO CREDITS: Cover, pp. 1, 3, 25, 34, 36—Barbara Marvis; p. 6—Nicholas Roerich; pp. 10, 22, 33—Sharon Beck; p. 14—Henry Fuseli; p. 20—Archive Photos/Getty Images; p. 28—Mansell/Time Life Pictures/Getty Images; p. 32—Ted Spiegel/National Geographic/Getty Images; p. 40—North Wind Photo Archives.

BIOGRAPHY FROM ANCIENT CIVILIZATIONS

LEGENDS, FOLKLORE, AND STORIES OF ANCIENT WORLDS

CONTENTS

*For Your Information

In *Guests from Overseas*, Nicholas Roerich painted Viking traders in the *kaupskip*. Vikings sailed all the known seas of their time, not just as sea raiders, but also as discoverers and traders.

CHAPTER ONE

THE VIKING AGE

"Lo, it is nearly three hundred and fifty years that we and our fathers have inhabited this most lovely land," wrote Alcuin the Anglo-Saxon scholar-monk of York, "and never before has such terror appeared in Britain as we have now suffered from a pagan race, nor was it thought that such an inroad from the sea could be made."[1] Alcuin was writing to Ethelred Moll, king of Northumbria, shortly after learning of the Viking raid on the tiny coastal isle of Lindisfarne in 793 CE. The raiders came from Hordaland, across the North Sea in southern Norway. They destroyed the monastery of St. Cuthbert and left it "spattered with the blood of the priests of God," continued Alcuin, "despoiled of all its ornaments; a place more venerable than all in Britain is given as a prey to pagan peoples."[2] Thus terror, slayings, and pillage ushered in what most historians regard as the start of the Viking Age.

The Viking Age began, flourished, and waned during the three centuries from 800 to 1100, give or take a few years at either end. Until recent times, historians and scholars generally regarded Vikings as cruel and brutal barbarians. Under the year 793, the *Anglo-Saxon Chronicle* recorded the arrival of the Vikings in England this way:

> In this year dire portents [omens] appeared over Northumbria and sorely frightened the people. They consisted of immense whirlwinds and flashes of lightning, and fiery dragons were

seen flying in the air. The great famine immediately followed those signs, and a little after that in the same year, on 8 June, the ravages of heathen men miserably destroyed God's church on Lindisfarne, with plunder and slaughter.[3]

Beyond question, many Vikings were indeed barbarians, both cruel and brutal. Many, in fact, possessed a number of other similarly distasteful qualities. But in light of modern archaeological discoveries, scholars have begun to recognize that Vikings were far more complex than their traditional barbaric image might suggest. Not only were they raiders and conquerors, they were also courageous explorers and enterprising colonists as well. So, who were these Vikings? Why did they leave their homelands to wreak terror in much of their known world? And where and how did they roam?

Scholars offer several sources for the name *viking*. One of the most logical origins of the word is the possible root *vik*, which means "an inlet, bay, or fjord" in the Old Norse (Scandinavian) language. To go *a-viking* meant to "sail off on a plundering raid." Anyone who did so was called a *vikingr*. Thus *viking* came to mean "a raider or pirate who lived in a fjord." In time, all Scandinavians—Norwegians, Swedes, and Danes—became known as Vikings. The name was sometimes extended to include the people of Finland and Iceland.

Other Europeans called the Scandinavian raiders by various other names, such as Northmen, Norsemen, or Danes. Those called Danes, however, did not necessarily come from Denmark. In Western Europe, folks of Charlemagne's Frankish empire referred to them as *Nordmanni* (Northmen or Normans). And the Slavs of Eastern Europe called the Swedish Vikings *Rus*, possibly from the Finnish name for Sweden, *Rotsi*. Russia eventually drew its name from the *Rus*. Europeans rarely referred to these men from the north as Vikings until after the Viking Age.

Why these northern sea raiders left their homes and began the Viking Movement late in the eighth century remains open to question. Historians at first thought that overpopulation and scarcity of land at home prompted them to seek improved conditions elsewhere. This may have held true for some areas of western Norway, but overcrowding and land shortages did not exist in Denmark and Sweden. Although many

An artist's rendering of the ruins of Lindisfarne serve as a stark reminder of a Viking raid that desecrated the Anglo-Saxon monastery founded by St. Aidan in 634. Vikings from nearby Norway carried out the raid in June 793 to open the Viking Age.

Scandinavians migrated during the Viking Age, few left home out of necessity. Rather, most of the first generations of Vikings set out for faraway places in search of wealth unavailable to them at home. Further, an increase in trade and the establishment of rich trading centers both in England and across Europe provided ample opportunity for plunder and the redistribution of wealth. At about the same time, Scandinavians developed new shipbuilding techniques that enabled them to sail farther and faster than ever before. And that is what they did.

The Vikings surged southward and plunged down upon England and northern Europe. They struck suddenly and by surprise, usually attacking undefended targets such as churches and markets rich in booty. Visiting their savagery upon the unsuspecting and the unready, they spread terror wherever they went. Parishioners of one French church called upon a Higher Power for protection: "*A furore Normannorum libera*

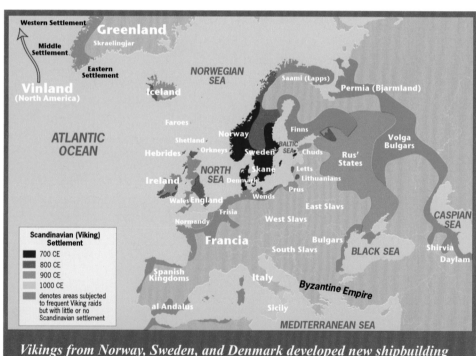

Vikings from Norway, Sweden, and Denmark developed new shipbuilding techniques that enabled them to voyage far and wide during the Viking Age (800–1100). They sailed ocean and inland waters, establishing settlements and raiding neighboring nations.

nos, Domine—From the fury of the Northmen deliver us, O Lord."[4] Thousands of Europeans repeated this simple prayer for the better part of three centuries.

Norwegians and Danes led the Viking assault on Western Europe, and the Swedes or *Rus* carved a ruthless path into the Slavic lands of Eastern Europe. As both plunderers and traders, their travels carried them far and wide. Their shallow-draft longships, fitted with both oars and sails, were sturdy and reliable on the open sea and capable of sailing swiftly upriver to inland settlements. In the words of Gwyn Jones, a noted scholar of Viking culture, the Vikings ranged "from the North Cape and White Sea to the Pillars of Hercules, from Newfoundland and Baffin Island to the Volga Bend and Byzantium."[5]

Despite their savage image, little evidence exists to suggest that the Vikings were any more violent or brutal than other warriors of their time in medieval Europe. Historic references to the English, Irish, Franks, and others of their day do not lack for blood and gore. Both the Vikings and their peers lived in turbulent times in which violence played a prominent role. Two things set the Vikings apart from their victims—the element of surprise made possible by attacks from the sea, and paganism. The worship of many gods by first-generation raiders allowed them to slaughter Christians and their clergy without care or compassion. But the image of such brutality often detracts from more constructive aspects of the Viking culture.

Vikings excelled at decorative arts. Violence aside, their poetry and prose sang of ideals such as honor and freedom. They traded as often as they raided, supplying such items as furs, walrus ivory and hide, seal skins, salted and dried fish, soapstone (talc), and falcons to consumers in Western Europe. In exchange, Viking trading ships known as *knörrs* returned home with cargoes of silver, wine, glass, fine pottery, and weapons from Western Europe, and silver and silks from Asia. In Eastern Europe, they navigated along rivers in eastern Russia and established trading networks extending from the Baltic to the Caspian and the Black Seas.

At a time when feudal Europe defined itself by various class distinctions—royals, nobles, merchants, artisans, peasants, serfs, and so on—Vikings characterized themselves as either free or unfree. Freemen ranged from kings and chiefs to tenant farmers and farm laborers. As in most societies, however, the wealthy enjoyed power and advantages over the poor.

Women had fewer legal rights than men and no political rights. Nevertheless, they achieved a status in Viking society far beyond the wildest imaginings of women elsewhere in medieval Europe. Wives owned land, operated farms, and kept their maiden names. Marriages were usually arranged, but wives could divorce their spouses by simply stating their intent to witnesses.

Not all Scandinavians went *a-viking*. Technically, only a small percentage of them could claim the name "Viking." Most were "part-time raiders" who worked at farming and other more peaceful occupations most of the time. Of those who voyaged to Europe and other places, many settled abroad and blended their unique northern culture with those of distant societies. Notable among their various settlements were those in the British Isles and France.

Alfred the Great eventually drove the Vikings out of England late in the ninth century. Charles III of France, known as Charles the Simple, ceded lands to the Vikings under Rollo, the first duke of Normandy, in 911. Not surprisingly, the lands later became known as Normandy. In the meantime, while Alfred was making life miserable for Viking conquerors in England, some of their countrymen were ranging farther west in the North Atlantic.

Around 860, a Viking called Gardar the Swede was blown off course by high winds during a voyage from Norway to the Hebrides, a group of islands off the coast of Scotland. He eventually made landfall on an island he named Gardarsholm (Gardar's Island). Shortly afterward, Floki Vilgerdarson, from Rogaland in Norway, led the first Viking attempt to settle the island. He renamed it Iceland. Floki's settlement failed, but Norwegian Ingolf Arnarson arrived on the island in 874. About 400 settlers followed. By 930, Vikings had claimed most of the arable land. About three decades later, around 960, one of the island's most famous residents arrived. His name was Eirik Thorvaldsson, but most everyone called him Erik the Red.

Viking Ships

The Viking Age began when Scandinavian adventurers left home to seek their fortunes in Europe and beyond. Superbly crafted ships provided their chief mode of transportation. Countless medieval hearts twinged with terror at the sight of a Viking ship crammed with Northmen. Once ashore, little in the path of these fearsome marauders escaped their fury.

"The number of ships increases, the endless flood of vikings never ceases to grow bigger," wrote the ninth-century monk Ermentarius of Noirmoutier (nwar-myoo-TYAY), a French island in the Bay of Biscay. "Everywhere Christ's people are the victims of massacre, burning, and plunder. The vikings over-run all that lies before them, and none can withstand them."[6]

Two basic types of vessels made up the increasing number of ships referred to by Ermentarius—the *langskip* (longship) and the *kaupskip* (trade ship). These are generic terms for warships and merchant ships, respectively. Vikings built all their ships out of oak and pine cut from the vast forests of Scandinavia. Ship sizes and appearances varied according to use.

Warships were long and narrow and drew very little water. They were powered by both oars and a large square sail. A sleek design and shallow draft enhanced their speed and enabled them to navigate far upriver. A warship carried anywhere from 15 to 30 or more sets of oars. Trade ships were shorter and broader and were generally powered mostly by sail. Warships ranged in length from 65 to 95 feet (20 to 29 meters); trade ships measured about 50 feet (15 meters) long. Widths of both types of vessels ran from 14.5 to 17.5 feet (4.4 to 5.3 meters).

Model of a Viking longship

A distinctive feature of Viking warships was a gracefully curved prow (front end). Its upward sweep often ended in the carved head of a dragon. Ships with such carvings were known as *drakkar* ("dragon") ships. The most popular type of trade ship was an all-purpose vessel called a *knörr*.

Thor, the god of physical strength, was probably the most popular of the Norse gods. In the twilight of the gods, he killed the Midgard Serpent (shown here) with his mighty hammer Mjöllnir.

CHAPTER
TWO

THE SAGA BEGINS

Not much is known about Erik the Red. Only the barest details of his turbulent life have survived the ages. Most of what little is known about him comes from two Icelandic tales, titled *The Saga of the Greenlanders* (c.1200) and *Erik the Red's Saga* (c.1265). Together, they are called *The Vinland Sagas*. These tales describe the Norse discovery and exploration of Greenland and North America in the late tenth and early eleventh centuries. Neither of the two tales reveals more than a footprint of Erik himself. Based on the highlights of his life, and recorded information about Viking history and culture, however, many of the voids in Erik's personal history can be filled in with a fair degree of certainty and credibility.

Erik's footprints in time began in Jaederen, Norway, about 950. Jaederen is a wild and desolate coastal area that forms a part of the Rogaland region of southwestern Norway. It is one of only three areas of level land found along the Norwegian coast. Its unprotected shores pose a hazard to mariners. Over time, many vessels have foundered along its rocky coastline. Wild and unforgiving lands such as Jaederen often spawn violent men to match their wildness. One such man was a Viking named Thorvald.

Thorvald, according to *Erik's Saga*, was "the son of Asvald Ulfsson, son of Ox-Thorir."[1] In the Norse tradition, Thorvald took his last name by suffixing his father's first name with "son." Thus his full name became

Thorvald Asvaldsson (Asvald's son). When Thorvald reached maturity, he sired a son with a spouse whose name has fallen through the cracks of time. Thorvald named the boy Erik (also spelled Eirik or Eric). Erik, in turn, took his last name from the first name of his father. His full name became Erik Thorvaldsson, but his fiery-red hair soon earned him the more popular nickname of Erik the Red.

In Erik's time, life was hard. Just staying alive served as an adventure in itself. Norway—whose name derives from the "North Way," a sheltered sea route to the north of Europe through a chain of coastal islands and reefs—did not exist as a single nation. Rather, it consisted of about a dozen chiefdoms or kingdoms. Some of the realms were ruled by Danes. Fishing, sea mammal hunting, and farming were the main occupations in the coastal area where Erik lived.

Vikings were also warriors, of course. Many of them went *a-viking* abroad from time to time. A raider's life often hinged on fair seas or the keen edge of a sword.

At home, separate interests and loyalties frequently led to conflict among rival factions. But whether wielding sword or battle-ax, or working with fishnet, harpoon, or plowshare, the Viking lifestyle demanded tough men who feared naught but the gods above.

During Erik's boyhood, most Vikings were pagans. They answered not to a single god but to many gods. The mightiest of all Norse gods was Odin, a member of the Aesir family of gods and grandson of the primeval god Buri. Odin ruled in Asgard, the home of the gods in the center of the world. Legend holds that the other gods served him as "children serve their father."[2] He shaped the world from the body of the giant Ymir and sent the sun and the moon spinning into orbit. Odin carved Ask and Embla—the first man and woman—from tree trunks and gave them life and breath to create the human race.

From his high seat called Hildskjalf, Odin could see and hear everything in the universe. Two ravens, Huginn ("thought") and Muminn ("memory"), sat on his shoulders. Now and again, they would fly out over the world and return to whisper all they knew in the mighty god's ears. Every now and then, in his continual search for wisdom, Odin would ride his eight-legged horse, Sleipnir, across the land, through the air, and on top of the waters for a closer look at the universe he ruled.

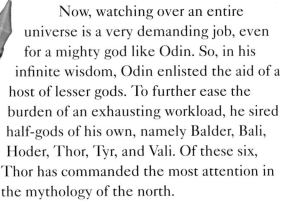

Odin

Now, watching over an entire universe is a very demanding job, even for a mighty god like Odin. So, in his infinite wisdom, Odin enlisted the aid of a host of lesser gods. To further ease the burden of an exhausting workload, he sired half-gods of his own, namely Balder, Bali, Hoder, Thor, Tyr, and Vali. Of these six, Thor has commanded the most attention in the mythology of the north.

Norse myths depict Thor as a massive, red-bearded warrior of enormous strength. Vikings looked upon him as the god of physical strength, thunder and lightning, rain and fair weather, and oaths. Farmers and sailors particularly looked to him for strength and guidance. Armed with his mighty hammer Mjöllnir, a pair of iron gloves, and a magic belt that doubled his strength, Thor defended gods and humans alike against the destructive force of a race of giants, the oldest creatures on earth. He was destined to play a critical role in the coming Ragnarök—the ultimate doom of the gods and the destruction of the world. (Ragnarök is often described as the "twilight of the gods.")

Norse mythology asserts that the forces of evil existing in the world will lead to its destruction. Odin, as high god and god of war, will lead his fallen warriors out of Valhalla—the "hall of the slain" in Asgard—to battle the giants and other evil forces. But Loki—the architect of all men's misfortunes—and his evil followers will defeat the gods in a great battle. Fenrir, a monstrous wolf, will swallow Odin. Thor will kill the great Midgard Serpent with his hammer, only to die himself from the serpent's venom. And fire and water will consume the gods. All's well that ends that way, however; after Ragnarök, a new world will arise. The gods will return to a world where happiness, wisdom, fertility, and goodness finally prevail. Or so the myths foretell.

Norse mythology accounts for many more gods than those already mentioned. Prominent among the Vanir family of gods was their leader Frey, god of fertility. Much like Odin, he controlled the sun and rain and thus the earth's fruitfulness. Farmers appealed to him for good harvests. He owned a magic ship, Skidbladnir, which was built by dwarves and always sailed before a following wind. It was large enough to contain all the gods, yet it could be folded to fit in his pocket. Fruitfulness, it seems, ran in Frey's family. His twin sister Freyja was goddess of love and perhaps the most famous of all Norse goddesses. She presided over marriage and fertility. Freyja frequently traveled in a chariot drawn by cats but also changed herself into a falcon and soared over her domain.

The Norse pantheon (entire group of gods) was amply populated with a god for almost any activity. Gods of the Aesir and Vanir families eventually united in Asgard to increase the lofty fold. But a vast array of gods does not constitute an organized religion. Pagans, by definition, do not believe in any of the world's chief—and thus called *organized*—religions. Vikings did not share a strict religious discipline. They recognized no universal doctrine or uniform method of worship. Believers chose their own god or gods and walked down separate paths to eternity, calling on different gods as their situations warranted.

Since Odin, the god of war, ranked as the high god among all Norse gods, he commanded the greatest following. His main role was to lead his followers into an end-all confrontation with evil—Ragnarök. True believers in Odin, it would seem, must anticipate and prepare for Ragnarök all their lives. It would further seem that preparing for war and destruction would breed violence and violent men. In any case, Erik the Red came to know both at a young age.

About 960, when Erik was ten years old, his father became involved in a violent neighborhood quarrel in Jaederen. A brawl ensued and at least two men were killed. Erik's father was sentenced to outlawry "because of manslaughters"[3] and banished from Jaederen for a period of three years. Thorvald Asvaldsson fled with his family to Iceland, where the "saga" of Erik the Red really begins.

Valhalla

In the time of Erik the Red, the Viking Age was on the wane. Pagan beliefs were yielding to Christian doctrines all across the northlands. But many Norsemen, including Erik, still clung to the old ways. They worshiped their various gods and aspired to a hero's welcome in Valhalla at the end of their days.

Valhalla, meaning "hall of the slain," is also known as Valhall or Valhöll. In Norse mythology, it is the great hall of the high god Odin in Asgard. In Valhalla, Odin gathers about him the souls of brave warriors who have fallen in battle. The dead warriors are called *einherjar* ("lone fighters"). They are chosen and led to the great hall by Valkyries, maiden warriors who dwell with Odin. Snorri Sturluson, a thirteenth-century Icelandic poet and historian, described the several tasks of the Valkyries this way: "Odin sends them to every battle; they allot death to men and decide on victory."[4] Once back in Valhalla, they "serve drink and take care of the tableware and drinking-vessels."[5]

The slain warriors eat boar's flesh and drink mead, a fermented beverage made of water and honey, malt, and yeast. Odin joins them but does not share in the feasting. He drinks only wine and eats no food, instead choosing to feed morsels to two wolves, Freki and Geri, who sit at his feet. The revelers sit under a roof thatched with spears, enclosed by walls bedecked with shields and coats of mail. At least 540 and up to 640 doors allow the warriors to exit rapidly when they pour forth each day to battle one another. Their battle will end only at the time of Ragnarök.

Many scholars picture Valhalla as a paradise for warriors in training for that one last great battle. Others have begun to interpret the great hall as a symbol of the grave. Erik the Red went to his own grave believing in the myth of Valhalla.

Odin with Freki and Geri at his feet

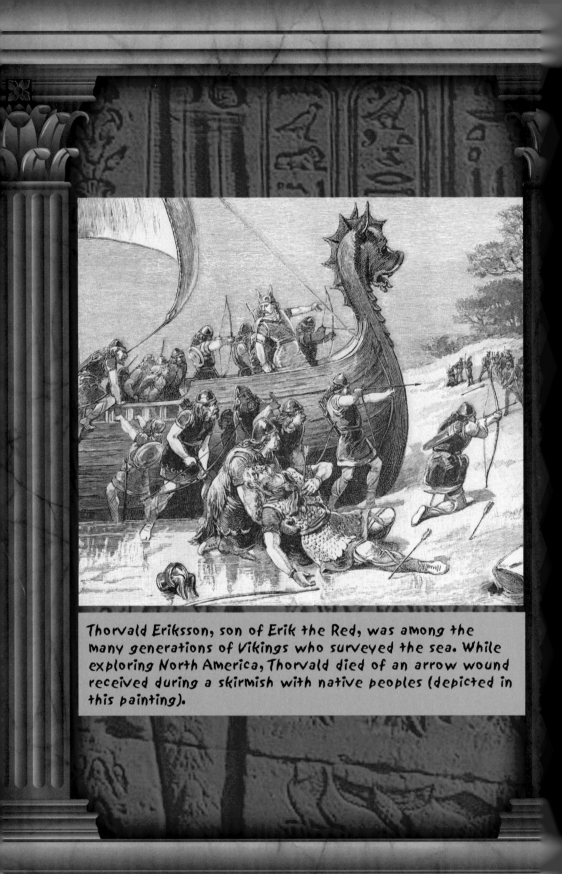

Thorvald Eriksson, son of Erik the Red, was among the many generations of Vikings who surveyed the sea. While exploring North America, Thorvald died of an arrow wound received during a skirmish with native peoples (depicted in this painting).

CHAPTER
THREE

ICELAND

Under a sentence of outlawry, Thorvald Asvaldsson fled from Norway with his family about 960. Other than identifying his son, *Erik the Red's Saga* makes no mention of the other members of Thorvald's family who went to Iceland with him. Neither does the story reveal any details of the brawl and slayings that brought the charges of manslaughter against Thorvald. Further, *Erik's Saga* does not define the *type* of outlawry sentence that Viking justice levied against him.

Two kinds of outlawry existed in Scandinavia in the Viking Age—lesser outlawry and full outlawry. Under a sentence of lesser outlawry, an offender retained some legal rights, and the period of exile was limited to three years. Full outlawry brought a life sentence, loss of all legal rights, and a permanent rejection from society. Thorvald may or may not have intended to return to Norway. Knowing either intention would give a clue to the severity of his sentence. But Thorvald's story, as related in *Erik's Saga*, ends almost as soon as it begins.

Precisely when and how Thorvald reached Iceland—and with whom—remains uncertain. After arriving in Iceland, according to the unknown author of *Erik's Saga*, Thorvald and Erik "occupied land in Hornstrandir, and dwelt at Drangar. There Thorvald died."[1] Unless further information about Thorvald surfaces, the world will never know the circumstances of his banishment or death. Even the question of why he elected to sail to Iceland remains unanswered.

Iceland's great snowfield Vatnajökull (Glacier of Rivers) covers more than eight percent of the island's surface. Hvannadalshnúkur, Iceland's highest peak (6,922 feet or 2,110 meters) is located in Vatnajökull's southern periphery. Reykjavík, the capital of Iceland, is the location of Ingolf Arnarson's settlement of 874.

Iceland is a roughly oval island about the size of Colorado, with a fjord-indented coastline of some 3,730 miles (6,000 kilometers). It lies about 570 miles (917 kilometers) west of Norway, across the rough waters of the Norwegian Sea. Its terrain consists mostly of tableland with an elevation averaging from 2,000 to 3,000 feet (610 to 914 meters). Lowlands form roughly one quarter of the island's landmass, only part of which is inhabitable. The great snowfield Vatnajökull covers some 3,247 square miles (8,410 square kilometers) of the island's southeastern corner. Only about one seventh of the land is arable. Historically, Iceland has suffered from destructive earthquakes, and more than 100 volcanoes loom there. Hornstrandir, where Thorvald and his family settled, lay along the rocky coast on the northwesternmost part of the island.

Some evidence suggests that Irish monks lived as hermits on Iceland before the Viking Age. Most historians credit Gardar the Swede with being the first Scandinavian to reach the island. Blown off course on a voyage from Norway to the Hebrides at the start of the 860s, Gardar discovered Iceland by chance. Reaching the island's Eastern Horn, he followed the coastline westward. He eventually encircled his discovery to prove it was an island, which he named Gardarsholm (Gardar's Island) after himself. Gardar spent the winter at Husavik, on the island's north coast. He returned to Norway in the spring.

News of Gardar's discovery reached Norwegian explorer Floki Vilgerdarson, who led a small party of settlers to Gardarsholm later in the 860s. His attempt to settle the island failed when he neglected to gather winter fodder and his livestock died. He renamed the island "Iceland." Disillusioned, Floki returned to Norway, but his name for the island stuck. Despite the coldness implied by the island's new name, two Norwegian foster-brothers, Ingolf and Hjorleif, set sail on an exploratory voyage to the island in the late 860s. The two brothers liked what they saw and returned about 870 to begin the first successful Norwegian settlement in Iceland.

Ingolf Arnarson and Hjorleif Hrodmundarson were sworn brothers. Like many Norsemen of their time, they had fled Norway after becoming involved in some killings. Upon their return to Iceland, Hjorleif settled at once at Hjorleifshofdi on the south coast. Ingolf called on the gods for guidance. He cast overboard the underpinnings of his high seat and vowed to settle only where the wood supports washed ashore. After searching for three years, he finally found the timbers at Reykjavík and built his homestead there. Meanwhile, Hjorleif had been killed by some slaves he had captured in Ireland. Ingolf tracked down the slaves and killed them during the first year. History has accorded Ingolf sole credit for the first successful settlement in Iceland in 874.

More settlers followed Ingolf to Iceland, mostly from western Norway, but also Scandinavians from Sweden, Denmark, and the Hebrides. By 930, most of the island's arable land had been claimed. At that time, the *Althing*—the lawmaking assembly of Iceland—was established at Thingvellir, 30 miles (48 kilometers) east of Reykjavík. Each community had a *Thing* (assembly), a self-governing body to handle

In an 1850 painting, artist Johann Peter Raadsig depicts Ingolf Arnarson, Iceland's first settler, arriving in what is now Reykjavík. Arnarson is shown directing workers as they erect pillars for his high seat. Several party members and a dog look on, while others unload a ship in the background.

local affairs. The *Althing* was an annual political assembly of all freemen that served as the governing body for the entire island. Ingolf's son Thorstein founded the first *Thing* in Iceland. Settlements were led by wealthy chieftains called *godar* (priests).

The settlements of Iceland and the Faroe Islands constitute the only permanent extensions of the Scandinavian world resulting from the Viking expansion. At the time of Thorvald's arrival in Iceland, Norwegian settlements there were less than a century old. Despite the rule of chieftains and the establishment of lawmaking assemblies, lawlessness and blood feuds played an ongoing role in the lives of Icelanders. Those twin scourges of early Icelandic society would not wait long to affect the life of Erik the Red.

As chronicled in *Erik the Red's Saga*, Erik's story jumps ahead in time to after the death of his father. At some unspecified point, he "then married Thjodhild."[2] Erik's new spouse was the daughter of Jorund Atlason and Thorbjorg the Ship-breasted. (In accord with the Nordic naming custom, her full name became Thjodhild Jorundardottir.) Thjodhild's mother Thorbjorg was married to Thorbjorn of Haukadal at the time of her daughter's marriage to Erik. After marrying, Erik and Thjodhild moved south. Erik cleared land at Haukadal and built a farm at Eiriksstadir (Erik's estate) near Vatnshorn. A run of bad luck befell Erik at Eiriksstadir.

It appears that somewhere along the line Erik had acquired some slaves, possibly captives from Viking raids on Ireland. In any case, some of his slaves caused a landslide to fall on the farm of a man named Valthjof at Valthjofsstadir (Valthjof's estate). Eyjolf the Foul, one of Valthjof's relatives, caught up with Erik's slaves near Skeidsbrekkur (the slopes above Vatnshorn) and killed them. Their murders touched off a blood feud.

In retaliation for the slaying of his slaves, Erik slew Eyjolf the Foul. Although it is unclear what part—if any—that Hrafn the Dueller had played in the incident, Erik also slew him at Leikskalar. Gerstein and

Shortly after marrying Thjodhild, Erik the Red and his new spouse settled in to this home in Eiriksstadir (Erik's estate) near Vatnshorn in Iceland.

Chapter THREE

Odd of Jorvi, Eyjolf's kinsmen, possibly intimidated by the permanent nature of Erik's retribution, accused Erik in court for Eyjolf's slaying. They made their case, and Erik was banished from Haukadal.

Erik then claimed Brokey and Oxney, islands in the Breidha Fjord, a bay on the northwest coast of Iceland. During his first winter in exile, he farmed at Tradir on the island of Sudurey. While there, he lent a man named Thorgest some bedstead boards. A bit later, Erik moved to Oxney and farmed at his old place at Eiriksstadir. He must have needed his old bedstead boards again, for he then asked Thorgest to return them. Thorgest, for whatever reason, did not return the boards. Erik was not one to take no for an answer when it came to reclaiming his property. He stomped over to Thorgest's place at Breidabolstad, seized the boards, and struck out for home. Thorgest chased him.

Thorgest caught up with Erik near his old farm at Drangar. The two hulking men and their comrades clashed in a terrible bloody brawl. Two of Thorgest's sons and several other men were killed in the fighting. After the fray, both Erik and Thorgest kept a large body of men about them. Styr and Eyjolf of Sviney, Thorbjorn Vifilsson, and the sons of Thorbrand of Alftafjord sided with Erik. In support of Thorgest, Thord Bellower and Thorgeir of Hitardal, along with Aslak of Langadal and his son Illugi, stepped forward. A *Thing* met at Thorsnes later and sentenced Erik and his companions to outlawry.

Erik told his friends that "he intended to seek out the land that Gunnbjorn, the son of Ulf Crow, had seen when he was driven off course westward and discovered Gunnbjarnarsker (Gunnbjorn's skerry [reef])."[3] Gunnbjorn had sighted the land to the west of Iceland about eighty years earlier. Erik prepared his ship for the westward voyage in Eiriksvog. Eyjolf hid him in Dimunarvog, while Thorgest and his cronies searched the islands for him.

With all in readiness, Erik loaded his family, followers, and slaves aboard his ship and bade farewell to friends who had opted to stay behind. He "promised to support them in any way he could if they should need his help."[4] Then, sometime in the year 982, Erik put to sea from Snaefellsnes, a peninsula in western Iceland, and sailed west into the dark waters of the North Atlantic.

Icelandic Law and Lawmakers

Icelanders created the *Althing* (general or national assembly) at Thingvellir around 930. Its founding marked the beginning of the Icelandic Commonwealth Period (930–1262). Iceland had no kings or central authorities or police during this time. Icelanders needed some means of making laws and enforcing them within the framework of a social contract. The *Althing* filled this void.

An Althing *meeting in Iceland*

The *Althing* met annually for two weeks in June at Thingvellir until 1798. It was then moved to Reykjavík. At its first meeting, the assembly established a national law for Iceland, adapted from the Gulathing law of southwest Norway. All freemen of the island nation, except those sentenced to outlawry, could attend the annual assembly. But all judicial and legislative power resided with thirty-six local chieftains called *godar* (singular *godi*). Only the *godar* could vote in the *Lögrétta*, the *Althing*'s legislative council. (The number of council members was raised to 39 in 965 and then to 48 in 1005; the *Althing* was abolished in 1800.) They elected a Lawspeaker, a president without executive power. His primary job was to recite the Icelandic Laws from the Law Rock, a raised spot at Thingvellir. Although the *godar* held near-absolute political power, they had to consider the opinions of their *thingmenn* (supporters). As freemen, the *thingmenn* could withdraw their support whenever they wished.

Beginning in 965, disputes that district *Things* (assemblies) could not resolve were heard at one of four "quarter" courts, named for Iceland's North, South, East, and West geographical quarters. A Fifth (High) Court was established to hear appeals of cases deadlocked in the quarter (lower) courts. The *godar* argued cases for their *thingmenn* at the *Althing*. In return, the *godar* could call upon the armed support of their *thingmenn* in blood feuds with other council members. Annual meetings at the *Althing* often turned into rather spirited affairs.

In this illustration, artist Carl Rasmussen portrays a Viking longboat with Erik the Red and his party sailing by an icebound land that became known as Greenland. History now credits Erik as the founder of the vast island's first European settlements.

CHAPTER
FOUR

GREENLAND

Erik the Red traced a westerly course across the cold and choppy waters of the Denmark Strait. He followed along the sixty-fifth parallel of north latitude, then coasted southward. Medieval storytellers who eventually recorded his saga neglected to describe his ship, but it was probably a *knörr* (a merchant vessel propelled by sail rather than by oars). After sailing for several days and about 450 miles, Erik sighted the inhospitable coast of the unknown land he sought. It lay under the glacier later called Hvitserk ("white shift"). Pack ice kept him from drawing close to the shore until he rounded a large jut of land that was soon to be known as Cape Farewell (Kap Farvel) in present-day Greenland (Kalaallit Nunaat).

Erik did not know it at the time, but he had reached the world's largest island (not counting Australia, which is classified as a continent). It measures about 1,650 miles (2,655 kilometers) in length, with a width of roughly 800 miles (1,285 kilometers). Two-thirds of the island lies north of the Arctic Circle, and ice covers 81 percent of its surface. The coastline looked bleak, and he sailed on. He had no choice.

Erik eventually came upon a part of the coast that was lined with sheltered fjords and mostly free of ice. It was also free of inhabitants. (The country's native Inuit population had departed long before Erik's arrival, probably because the climate had become too warm for them during a warming cycle.) Conditions in this new land, as Erik was soon to discover, compared favorably with those of Norway and held the promise of growth and prosperity.

Erik, no doubt, felt elated at the sight of this promising new land. Viking scholar Gwyn Jones described Erik's moment of discovery this way: "The rugged islands of the archipelago, the fjords and headlands, the hills right back to the Ice Cap, the rivers and lakes, and best of all the grassy slopes and scrub-strewn nooks, were his for the taking, and without loss of time he took them."[1] Compared to the rocky, barely arable lands Erik had known in Iceland, this new land must have looked like some kind of paradise indeed. He spent the next three years—the period of his banishment for outlawry—exploring the unnamed land.

Erik's explorations carried him along the southwestern coast of the island from Herjolfnes (Ikigait) to Eiriksfjord (Tunugdliarfik). During his wanderings, he and his party gave names to places and marked out sites for future farms and homes. He found the land rich in wildlife, with an abundance of bears, foxes, and caribou. A profusion of sea mammals populated the *skaergaard*—the rocky coastline sheltered by offshore islands and skerries (reefs). Wherever he found water, he found fish. And fowls aplenty filled the air everywhere he roamed.

Erik passed the first winter at Eiriksey Island, near the site of the later colony known as the Eastern Settlement. (Despite its name, the Eastern Settlement was located on the south*west* coast, just beyond Cape Farewell. It was actually the eastern*most* of three Norse settlements on Greenland.) The next spring, he moved to the head of Eiriksfjord, where he settled. That summer, he toured the unpeopled western regions. Erik spent the second winter in Eiriksholmar (Erik's small island), near Hvarfsgnipa. He passed the following summer on a voyage that carried him as far north as Snaefell and into Hrafnsfjord. Erik weathered the third winter of his exile back at Eiriksey, at the mouth of Eiriksfjord, before setting sail for Iceland the next summer.

Erik arrived back at Breidha Fjord, bursting with enthusiasm for the land he had just left, and eager to colonize it. He named the land Greenland, "because," he said, "men will desire much more to go there if the land has a good name."[2] In Erik's defense, his reference to the "green" of the land was more than just a ploy to encourage future settlers. A summertime visitor to Greenland can still find much green in the land, especially along the country's coastal fjords and across the inland valleys of its southwestern region.

Before getting on with his life, Erik had an old score to settle. He wintered with Ingolf at Holmlatur, then looked up his old enemy Thorgest in the spring. "Thorgest and he fought," according to *Erik's Saga*, "and [Erik] met with defeat. After that they were reconciled."[3] The unknown storyteller left out any details of their encounter, but Thorgest must have been a brute of a man indeed to have subdued the likes of Erik the Red.

With his blood feud with Thorgest ended at last, Erik concentrated on assembling a sizable party of colonists to return with him to Greenland. Conditions in Iceland aided his efforts. Icelanders were still recovering from a famine that had devastated the island a decade earlier. All the habitable land had long since been claimed, and prospects for both rich and poor looked bleak. Encouraging them to accept the risks of starting a new life in Greenland proved easier than Erik had imagined. He quickly put together a fleet of twenty-five ships and sailed again for his new homeland in about 985.

Of the 25 ships that left Iceland with Erik, 14 rounded Cape Farewell and arrived safely in the sheltered fjords of what is now Qaqortoq. Eleven vessels either turned back or were lost in the often rough and ice-filled waters between Iceland and Greenland. Such losses reflected the dangers of ocean crossings in northern waters. Yet, to many, being among the first to claim new lands and build better futures offset the risks. Viking ships likely to have made the voyage carried about thirty people or slightly more. Estimates of the actual number of people who survived the crossing range from 400 to 500. Most of the colonists were probably wealthy chieftains or merchants, affluent enough to afford their own ships.

In Qaqortoq, the Icelanders found a safe harbor, fine fishing, and excellent pasturelands. There they established the Eastern Settlement, called Eystribyggo. Erik, who had already selected the most favorable sites for himself, built a farmstead at the head of Eiriksfjord named Brattahlid. Traditional Norse longhouses and cow barns sprang up all around the area. Farms in the Eastern Settlement numbered more than 190.

As the founder of Greenland's first European settlements, Erik the Red naturally selected a choice piece of real estate upon which to build his own dwellings. He called the site of his new home Brattahlid. The remains of three farmsteads, a **Thing,** *and a stone church can still be seen there.*

Some of Erik's original settlers, along with groups of latecomers to Greenland, sailed on up the coast about 300 miles (480 kilometers) to present-day Nuuk, or Godthaab, and founded the Western Settlement, called Vestribyggo. About ninety farms prospered there. Others established a cluster of some twenty farms about halfway between the two larger settlements. Although generally considered a part of the Western Settlement, these farmsteads were unofficially known as the Middle Settlement.

All three settlements offered good farmland, particularly the Western Settlement, with its lush grasslands and stands of dwarfed trees. Its lakes and rivers teemed with fish, migratory harp seals occasioned past in abundance, and its vast uplands abounded with caribou. It was also closer to the northerly hunting grounds called Nordsetur, where great numbers of walrus frolicked in the icy waters and across the floes.

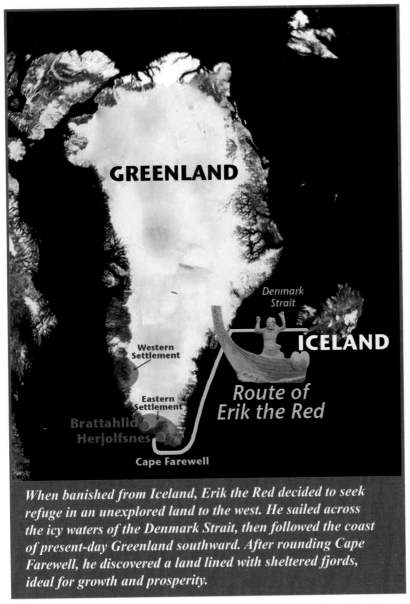

GREENLAND

Denmark
Strait

ICELAND

Western
Settlement

Eastern
Settlement

Route of
Erik the Red

Brattahlid
Herjolfsnes

Cape Farewell

When banished from Iceland, Erik the Red decided to seek refuge in an unexplored land to the west. He sailed across the icy waters of the Denmark Strait, then followed the coast of present-day Greenland southward. After rounding Cape Farewell, he discovered a land lined with sheltered fjords, ideal for growth and prosperity.

In such settings, Erik and the settlers he led survived by farming and hunting. They raised cattle, hogs, and sheep; they hunted bears, caribou, walrus, and other animals. Trade became an important part of their subsistence. They traded furs and hides, ropes and cables, oil, woolens, sea-ivory, polar bears, and falcons for necessities such as corn, iron (including wrought weapons), timber, European-style clothes

Present-day Nuuk (or Godthaab) is the site of Erik the Red's Western Settlement. The modern town provides a home for more than 12,000 hardy inhabitants. Fish processing and scientific research stations are their chief means of earning a living.

(usually from Norway), and various luxury items. Life in Greenland was difficult at best, but it was likely better than what most of Erik's settlers had known in Iceland.

In his new leadership role, Erik the Red's social standing rose from simple farmer (and convicted criminal) to paramount chieftain of Greenland. He played a prominent part in the first Greenlandic *landnám*, the parceling out of new lands among the settlers. Brattahlid became the political center of the Eastern Settlement. The Greenlanders quickly formed an *Althing* and adopted a constitution based on the Icelandic model. Little is known about Erik's role in the new government, but some scholars believe he may have served as Greenland's first Lawspeaker.

As a kind of "gentleman farmer" in Greenland, Erik the Red found a peace of mind he had seldom known before. With so many days of violence behind him at last, he also found time to raise a family.

Brattahlid

Erik the Red did not discover Greenland, but he gave the world's largest island its name. And scholars universally recognize him as its founder. As the first European to explore the island in depth and at length, Erik understandably laid claim to one of its nicest areas to start his farmstead and begin his new life. He called his new home Brattahlid.

Erik built Brattahlid, which means "steep slope," on a sharp incline overlooking Eiriksfjord. Greenland's inner fjords offered Erik and his settlers sheltered land and open space for farming. Most of the land was bare of trees, particularly in the Eastern Settlement, so the Norse colonists built their houses of turf and stone and lined them with driftwood. Between the ninth and twelfth centuries, the North Atlantic region experienced a warming trend. The climate then was milder and better suited to habitation than are the harsher environmental conditions of the present. Today, the waters of Eiriksfjord remain frozen from October to May.

Brattahlid, now known by its Inuit name Qagssiarsuk ("Little Strange Creek"), became the center of societal activities for the Norse Greenlanders in the Eastern Settlement. Erik was a gracious host. More than once he opened his house to guests for an entire winter. Erik's hospitality lends further insight into his transformation from a man of considerable violence to a community leader of somewhat gentler ways.

Today, visitors to the Eastern Settlement can still see the remains of three large farmsteads, the site of a *Thing*, and a stone church. One of the farm complexes has become popularly known as "Erik the Red's farm." Nearby, the remains of a small turf church have been excavated in modern times at Brattahlid. Experts believe them to be those of the church founded by Thjodhild, Erik's wife, after her

Thingvellir, the site of the first Althing

conversion to Christianity in the late tenth century (see chapter 5). Most of the surviving stone structures date from the thirteenth and fourteenth centuries, long after Erik's time.

This statue of Leif Eriksson, son of Erik the Red, stands in Reykjavik, the capital of Iceland, to commemorate his discovery of North America. Leif's voyage of discovery preceded that of Christopher Columbus by almost 500 years.

CHAPTER
FIVE

THE STUFF OF LEGENDS

History has begrudgingly surrendered only bits and scraps of information about the life of Erik the Red. There seems little doubt, however, that he was a rowdy, brawling, seafaring adventurer and explorer. He lived a hard life in harsh places in hard times. Given his extreme lifestyle, some may wonder how he managed to father and raise four children. Others may marvel at his remarkable turnabout from outlaw to respectable and respected community leader in the twilight of a riotous life. Yet the twists and turns of real life routinely exceed those of fiction's make-believe scenarios. And so it happened that the exceptional life of Erik the Red proved the rule.

"Eirik the Red farmed at Brattahlid," recounts *The Saga of the Greenlanders*. "There he was held in the highest esteem, and everyone deferred to his authority."[1] The unknown storyteller neglects to include any mention of what Erik did to gain the esteem and deference of his fellow colonists in Greenland. He must have done a lot of good for the people of his community. A man does not earn the admiration of his peers and attract a following for no reason. Too often, good deeds go underreported. In judging Erik's character, his implied virtues should be carefully balanced against his well-defined wrongdoings. About five hundred Greenlanders found the goodness in him. Four of them were his children.

"Eirik's children were Leif, Thorvald, Thorstein and a daughter, Freydis,"[2] the Greenlander's tale continues. Here, again, the unnamed tale-spinner leaves out important details of Erik's family life, omitting when and where the children were born, or even the order of their births. Some scholars name Leif as Erik's second son and relate that he was born near present-day Budardalur, a small village in northwest Iceland. (It was Leif who later replaced Erik as the paramount chieftain of Greenland.) Thorvald appears to have been the first son of Erik and Thjodhild, which would make Thorstein their third. Freydis, according to *Erik's Saga*, was Erik's "illegitimate daughter,"[3] making her a half sister to the three boys. Any hint as to her mother's identity goes unmentioned.

Of Erik's three sons, Leif Eriksson (also Erikson or Ericsson) is far and away the most famous. Historians widely credit him with leading the first European expedition to the mainland of North America. Leif was born in Iceland about 980. At the age of two, he sailed for Greenland with his family, which likely then consisted of his father and mother and his older brother Thorvald. Leif's boyhood years in Greenland have gone unrecorded until he reached the age of about nineteen.

In the summer of 999, Leif sailed to Norway and was converted to Christianity in the court of King Olaf I Tryggvason (who reigned from 995 to 1000). Olaf had introduced Christianity to Norway at the end of the tenth century. He called upon Leif, notes *The Norse Discovery of America*, to spread his new faith to Greenland, saying "in thy hands the cause will surely prosper."[4] Leif sailed back to Greenland in the spring and converted his mother and numerous others to Christianity.

Thjodhild "embraced the faith promptly, and caused a church to be built at some distance from the house."[5] The turf-walled structure became known as Thjodhild's Church. Its foundation was unearthed at Brattahlid in the 1960s. Erik the Red did not share Thjodhild's fervor for the new religion and remained true to his pagan gods. As a result, after her conversion, she refused to share her bed with her husband, "whereat he was sorely vexed."[6]

Several years earlier, as recorded in *The Saga of the Greenlanders*, a merchant named Bjarni Herjolfsson set out from Iceland on a voyage to Greenland and was "beset by winds from the north and fog."[7] He and his crew became lost. When the sun came out again after many days, they sighted a strange land. They followed its shoreline north in search of Greenland and found a second and third land before reaching their original destination. Bjarni told Erik the Red and numerous other Greenlanders of his sightings. When Leif Eriksson returned home from Norway, he heard "much talk of looking for new lands."[8] He immediately looked up Bjarni, bought his ship, and prepared to sail to the west in search of those lands.

Leif invited his father to lead this new voyage of discovery. Even at his advancing age, Erik the Red remained one of the finest navigators to have ever sailed the ice-filled waters of the north. No one knew that better than Leif. Erik still felt the lure of the sea and faraway places, but he complained of growing old. He could not bear the wet and the cold as he had in days long past. Leif persisted. He told his aging parent that he "still commanded the greatest good fortune of all his kinsmen."[9] In the end, Erik gave in to his son's urgings and agreed to go.

On the day of their scheduled departure, probably in the year 1000, Erik the Red set out from his farm on horseback to join his son at portside in Eiriksfjord. When he drew within sight of the ship, his horse stumbled and threw him. The old Viking fell hard and injured his foot. Leif rushed to aid his fallen father. Erik said to him: "I am not intended to find any other land than this one where we now live. This will be the end of our travelling together."[10] Erik returned to Brattahlid to take care of his injury. Because of a freak accident, a new and exciting chapter in North American history would be written without him.

Leif and a crew of thirty-five sailed along the coast of North America, exploring and naming Helluland (Flat Rock Land), Markland (Forest Land), and Vinland (Vine or Wine Land). Today, these lands are generally thought to be Baffin Island, Labrador, and Newfoundland, respectively. In Vinland, they built shelters and spent the winter. Because of the explorations of Leif and his crew, most historians credit them as being the first Europeans to actually land on the North American continent.

On the voyage home in the spring, Leif sighted a group of fifteen sailors who had become shipwrecked on a coastal skerry. He hailed them and learned that they were Norsemen. Their leader was a man named Thorir. Inviting them aboard his ship, Leif told them to bring "as much of

The above rendering portrays Leif Eriksson and his landing party off the coast of Vinland. Small ships, and smaller landing boats, required great courage and even greater navigational skills for the Vikings to stay alive in the frigid and choppy waters of the North Atlantic.

your valuables as the ship can carry."[11] They all arrived safely at Brattahlid. Leif's alert sighting of the Norsemen had proved most fortunate for them. But it was their savior who earned the nickname "Leif the Lucky" for his part in their rescue. The name stuck with Leif for the rest of his life.

At Brattahlid, Leif invited Thorir, along with his wife Gudrid and three other men, to spend the winter with him there. He also arranged places to stay for the rest of both his own and Thorir's crew members. By then, Leif, like his father, had become very wealthy and much respected. But Leif's luck, and the luck of his rescued guests, soon turned bad.

That winter, a great sickness fell upon Brattahlid. A fever struck down Thorir and most of his crew. And, as so understated in *The Saga of the Greenlanders*, "Eirik the Red also died that winter."[12] Those seven words—simple, stark, and written almost as an afterthought—abruptly conclude the life of one of history's most fascinating characters. A brawler and a rogue, an outlaw and an explorer, a father and a nation builder, Erik the Red was all these things and more. History will perhaps always best remember him as the founder of Greenland and the father of Leif Eriksson.

Over the next several centuries, the settlements that Erik the Red founded grew in population from something over 400 people to about 4,000. Sometime in the fifteenth century, Greenland's Norse population mysteriously vanished. An account written by Norwegian cleric Ivar Bardarson, probably in 1364, ominously states: "*Skraeling* [a derogatory term for native populations] have destroyed all the Western Settlement. There is an abundance of horse, goats, bulls, and sheep, all wild, and no people neither Christian nor heathen."[13] The last positive indication of Norse existence in Greenland is a marriage record in a church in the Eastern Settlement dating to 1403.

Scientists and scholars offer several reasons for the demise of Norse Greenland. Some suggest that the Inuit Greenlanders reclaimed the vast island when the climate turned cold again. Others suggest that the Norse settlers became increasingly isolated from Norway, while failing to adapt themselves to Greenland's harsh environment (as had the Inuit). They clung stubbornly to their traditional Norse lifestyle in a land that just as stubbornly refused to accept their ways. Still others suggest that pests might have wreaked havoc on their crops, or that pestilence might have doomed them to an early extinction.

Whatever the reason for their demise, the Norse Greenlanders faded into history's archives and by the mid-1400s were all but forgotten. But the fiery image of their first leader and the founder of Norse Greenland lives on. And perhaps somewhere in Valhalla, Odin and all the lesser gods smile upon Erik the Red, for in death he has become the stuff of legends. As for Erik's son, Leif—well, that's a whole other story.

Thjodhild's Church

In the summer of 999, Leif Eriksson sailed to Norway and spent the winter in the court of King Olaf I Tryggvason. King Olaf, who had just introduced Christianity to Norway, converted young Leif into his newly adopted religion. Olaf asked his new convert to urge Christianity upon the settlers back in Greenland. This Leif did. Perhaps his chief convert was his own mother, Thjodhild Jorundardottir.

Thjodhild promptly embraced Christianity with uncommon vigor. Erik the Red did not share her enthusiasm. She tried hard to convert him to the religion of Christ, but her husband kept his lifetime beliefs in the pagan gods of the Norse. Thjodhild cajoled and threatened him. Share my commitment to Christ, she told him, or stay out of my bed. Erik faced a tough choice, but he clung fast to Odin and the rest. From then on, the master of Brattahlid slept alone—and not too happily.

Thjodhild—perhaps hoping that a congregation of Christians might persuade her husband to join them in worship—built a church. She built it at Brattahlid in c.1001, not too close to the farmhouse. (Erik the Red was probably still grumbling about his altered marital arrangement.) The tiny church, built of turf and lined with wood, measured about seven feet by eleven feet (two meters by three and one-half meters). Its two long interior walls were slightly convex

in the style of Scandinavian houses of the time. Low benches along each wall accommodated a small gathering of worshipers. Erik the Red was not one of them.

Reconstruction of Thjodhild's church

Thjodhild's Church, as it was named, was the first Christian church on the western side of the Atlantic. In 1961, excavators found the remains of the church and a small cemetery outside the church containing the graves of more than one hundred men, women, and children. Erik the Red might have been laid to rest outside Thjodhild's Church—but then again, maybe not.

CHAPTER NOTES

Chapter 1. The Viking Age
1. John Marsden, *The Fury of the Northmen: Saints, Shrines and Sea-raiders in the Viking Age, A.D. 793–878* (New York: St. Martin's Press, 1995), p. 34.
2. Ibid.
3. William M. Fitzhugh and Elisabeth I. Ward (editors), *Vikings: The North Atlantic Saga* (Washington, D.C.: Smithsonian Institution Press, 2000), p. 127.
4. Patricia S. Daniels and Stephen G. Hyslop, *Almanac of World History* (Washington, D.C.: National Geographic Society, 2003), p. 127.
5. Gwyn Jones, *A History of the Vikings* (Rev. Ed., New York: Oxford University Press, 1984), p. 1.
6. Ibid., p. 215.

Chapter 2. The Saga Begins
1. Örnólfur Thorsson (editor), *The Sagas of the Icelanders: A Selection* (New York: Penguin Books, 2001), p. 654.
2. John Haywood, *Encyclopedia of the Viking Age* (New York: Thames & Hudson, 2000), p. 137.
3. Project Gutenberg: *Eirik the Red's Saga* http://www.gutenberg.org/files/17946/17946-h/17946-h.htm, p. 3.
4. Andy Orchard, *Dictionary of Norse Myth and Legend* (London: Cassell, 1997). p. 172.
5. Ibid.

Chapter 3. Iceland
1. Project Gutenberg: *Eirik the Red's Saga* http://www.gutenberg.org/files/17946/17946-h/17946-h.htm, p. 3.
2. Ibid.

3. "Eirik the Red's Saga" in Örnólfur Thorsson (editor), *The Sagas of the Icelanders: A Selection* (New York: Penguin Books, 2001), pp. 654–655.
4. Ibid., p. 655.

Chapter 4. Greenland
1. Gwyn Jones, *A History of the Vikings* (Rev. Ed., New York: Oxford University Press, 1984), p. 290.
2. Project Gutenberg: *Eirik the Red's Saga* http://www.gutenberg.org/files/17946/17946-h/17946-h.htm, p. 4.
3. Ibid.

Chapter 5. The Stuff of Legends
1. "The Saga of the Greenlanders" in Örnólfur Thorsson (editor), *The Sagas of the Icelanders: A Selection* (New York: Penguin Books, 2001), p. 636.
2. Ibid.
3. Ibid., p. 666.
4. The Internet Sacred Text Archive: *The Norse Discovery of America* (Chapter II: "The Saga of Erik the Red"), p. 42. http://www.sacred-texts.com/neu/nda/nda06.htm
5. Ibid., p. 43.
6. Ibid.
7. Thorsson, p. 637.
8. Ibid., p. 638.
9. Ibid.
10. Ibid.
11. Ibid., p. 641.
12. Ibid.
13. William M. Fitzhugh and Elisabeth I. Ward (editors), *Vikings: The North Atlantic Saga* (Washington, D.C.: Smithsonian Institution Press, 2000), p. 327.

CHRONOLOGY

950   Erik the Red (Eirik Thorvaldsson) is born in Jaederen in southwestern Norway.

960   He flees to Iceland with his outlawed father, Thorvald Asvaldsson.

960–980   Historical records fail to document precise dates concerning Erik the Red for this score of years, but several defining events in his life occur during this period: his father dies; shortly thereafter, Erik marries Thjodhild; their marriage ultimately produces three sons, Leif Eriksson, Thorvald, and Thorstein; Erik also sires an illegitimate daughter, Freydis. Two incidents of violence result in Erik's conviction for the slaying of three men and thus his later eviction from Iceland for a three-year period.

981   Banished from Iceland on outlawry charges for manslaughter, Erik sails west to a mysterious and unknown land he names Greenland.

982   He begins a three-year exploration of Greenland.

985   Erik discovers Disko (Qeqertarsuaq) Island in the Davis Strait on the west coast of Greenland.

986   He returns to Iceland. He sails from Iceland with 25 ships and about 500 colonists to establish the first settlements in Greenland. Only 14 ships reach Greenland. Survivors form the nucleus of two Icelandic colonies, the Western and Eastern Settlements on the west coast of Greenland.

999   Erik's son Leif voyages to Norway and spends the winter in the court of Norway's Christian king, Olaf I; Leif and his mother, Thjodhild, adopt Christianity; Erik does not.

1001   Leif Eriksson returns from the Vinland voyage. Erik dies at Brattahlid.

Puffins in Iceland

874	Ingolf Arnarson establishes first successful settlement in Iceland.
900	Vikings raid along the Mediterranean coast. Maya civilization in Mexico and Central America collapses.
907	Tang Dynasty collapses and epoch of the Five Dynasties begins in China (to 960).
911	King Charles III (Charles the Simple) of France cedes land, later named Normandy, to the Vikings.
920	Byzantine Empire is extended to the Tigris and Euphrates Rivers.
935	Arabs found the city of Algiers in North Africa.
939	Revolts against imperial rule ignite a period of civil war lasting until 1185 in Japan.
941	Rus (Swedish) Vikings attack Constantinople (Istanbul).
944	The Irish sack Dublin.
961	Vikings sack St. Paul's Cathedral of London.
962	Hospice of St. Bernard is founded at St. Bernard's Pass in Switzerland. Otto I is crowned Holy Roman Emperor.
978	Building of St. Mark's Basilica begins in Venice after it burned down in 976.
983	Venice and Genoa carry on flourishing trade between Asia and Western Europe.
991	Ethelred II pays first Danegeld (tribute) to stop Danish attacks on England.
993	Canonization of saints begins.
995	Olaf I (Olaf Tryggvason) defeats Danes and conquers Norway; he proclaims it a Christian kingdom.
1000	Olaf I is killed in the battle of Svold against Svein Forkbeard; Danes reclaim rule of Norway. Leif Eriksson, son of Erik the Red, explores the coast of North America. Chinese perfect their invention of gunpowder.
1009	Muslims sack the Holy Sepulcher in Jerusalem.
1013	Danes under Svein Forkbeard conquer England; Ethelred II flees to Normandy.
1015	Vikings abandon the Vinland settlement on the coast of North America.
1040	Macbeth murders Duncan of Scotland and becomes king (to 1057).
1042	Edward the Confessor rules England with the support of the Danes; Viking threat ends.
1045	Rodrigo Díaz de Vivar, the Spanish national hero known as El Cid ("the Lord"), is born.
1048	Omar Khayyam, Persian poet and scientist, is born.
1050	The city of Oslo is founded in Norway.

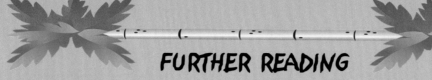

FURTHER READING

For Young Adults

Boyer Binns, Tristan. *The Vikings*. Mankato, MN: Compass Point Books, 2006.

Gassos, Dolores. *The Vikings*. Ancient Civilizations Series. New York: Chelsea House, 2005.

Landau, Elaine. *Exploring the World of the Vikings with Elaine Landau*. Exploring Ancient Civilizations with Elaine Landau Series. Berkeley Heights, NJ: Enslow Publishers, 2005.

Lassieur, Allison. *Lords of the Sea: The Vikings Explore the North Atlantic*. Mankato, MN: Capstone Press, 2006.

———. *Vikings*. Farmington Hills, MI: Lucent Books/Gale, 2001.

Mattern, Joanne. *Leif Eriksson: Viking Explorer*. Explorers! Series. Berkeley Heights, NJ: Enslow Publishers, 2004.

Works Consulted

Arbman, Holger. *The Vikings*. Translated and edited with an introduction by Alan Binns. New York: Barnes & Noble, 1995.

Batey, Colleen, Helen Clarke, R. I. Page, and Neil S. Price. *Cultural Atlas of the Viking World*. Edited by James Graham-Campbell. New York: Facts on File, 1994.

Batey, Colleen E., Judith Jesch, and Christopher D. Morris, eds. *The Viking Age in Caithness, Orkney and the North Atlantic*. Edinburgh, Scotland: Edinburgh University Press, 1995.

Bedini, Silvio A., ed. *Christopher Columbus and the Age of Exploration: An Encyclopedia*. New York: Da Capo Press, 1998.

Bohlander, Richard E., ed. *World Explorers and Discoverers*. New York: Da Capo Press, 1998.

Daniels, Patricia S., and Stephen G. Hyslop. *National Geographic Almanac of World History*. Washington, D.C.: National Geographic Society, 2003.

Davidson, H. R. Ellis. *Viking & Norse Mythology*. New York: Barnes & Noble, 1996.

Edmonds, Jane, ed. *Oxford Atlas of Exploration*. New York: Oxford University Press, 1997.

Fitzhugh, William W., and Elisabeth I. Ward, eds. *Vikings: The North Atlantic Saga*. Washington, D.C.: Smithsonian Institution Press, 2000.

Griffith, Paddy. *The Viking Art of War*. London: Greenhill Books, 1995.

Haywood, John. *Encyclopaedia of the Viking Age*. New York: Thames & Hudson, 2000.

———. *The Penguin Historical Atlas of the Vikings*. New York: Penguin Books, 1995.

Heath, Ian. *The Vikings*. Illustrated by Angus McBride. London: Osprey Publishing, 1999.

Jones, Gwyn. *A History of the Vikings*. Rev. ed. New York: Oxford University Press, 1984.

Kemp, Peter, ed. *The Oxford Companion to Ships and the Sea*. New York: Oxford University Press, 1988.

Marsden, John. *The Fury of the Northmen: Saints, Shrines and Sea-raiders in the Viking Age*. New York: St. Martin's Press, 1995.

Novaresio, Paolo. *The Explorers: From the Ancient World to the Present*. New York: Stewart, Tabori & Chang, 1996.

Orchard, Andy. *Dictionary of Norse Myth and Legend*. London: Cassell, 1997.

Page, R. I. *Chronicles of the Vikings: Records, Memorials and Myths*. New York: Barnes & Noble, 1995.

Salentiny, Fernand. *Encyclopedia of World Explorers: From Armstrong to Shackleton*. Edited by Werner Waldmann. London: Dumont Monte, 2003.

Sawyer, P. H. *Kings and Vikings: Scandinavia and Europe, A.D. 700–1100*. New York: Barnes & Noble, 1994.

Sawyer, Peter, ed. *The Oxford Illustrated History of the Vikings*. New York: Oxford University Press, 1997.

Thorsson, Örnólfur, ed. *The Sagas of Icelanders: A Selection.* New York: Penguin Books, 2001.

Toyne, S. M. *The Scandinavians in History.* New York: Barnes & Noble, 1996.

Wilson, David M. *The Vikings and Their Origins: Scandinavia in the First Millennium.* New York: Thames & Hudson, 1991.

On the Internet

Modern History Sourcebook: *The Discovery of North America by Leif Eriksson, c. 1000, from* The Saga of Erik the Red, *1387* http://www.fordham.edu/halsall/mod/1000Vinland.html

PBS: *The Viking Deception*
http://www.pbs.org/wgbh/nova/vinland

Reeves, Arthur Middleton, North Ludlow Beamish, and Rasmus B. Anderson. *The Norse Discovery of America,* "A Brief History of Erik the Red"
http://www.sacred-texts.com/neu/nda/nda08.htm

Sephton, John, translator. *The Project Gutenberg eBook of* Eirik the Red's Saga, *by Anonymous*
http://www.gutenberg.org/files/17946/17946-h/17946-h.htm

GLOSSARY

Althing—The lawmaking assembly of Iceland.

archipelago (ar-keh-PEH-leh-goh)—A group of islands.

Asgard—The home of the Norse gods in the center of the world.

Eiriksstadir—"Erik's estate"; one of Erik the Red's homes in Iceland.

Eystribyggo (es-tree-BEE-jo)—Eastern Settlement.

godar—Priests; wealthy chieftains who served on the sectional or national *Thing*.

Gardarsholm—"Gardar's Island"; original name for Greenland, named after its discoverer.

Jaederen (JED-uhr-en)—Section in southwest Norway where Erik the Red was born.

Kalaallit Nunaat (ka-LOT-leet new-NOT)—Present Inuit name for Greenland.

landnám—The parceling out of new lands among settlers.

Lindisfarne—Island off northern England; site of early Viking raid.

Lögrétta—Legislative council of the *Althing*.

pagan (PAY-gun)—Heathen; one who believes in many gods or has little or no religion.

Ragnarök—In Norse mythology, the last battle of the gods.

Reykjavík (ray-KYAH-veek)—Capital of Iceland.

Rogaland—County of southwest Norway, which encompasses Jaederen.

skraeling (SKREL-ing)—Derogatory Norse term for native peoples of Greenland and North America.

Thing—Assembly; a self-governing body to handle local affairs.

thingmenn—Supporters (constituents) of the *godar*.

Thingvellir—Site of the first *Althing* in Iceland.

Vestribyggo (ves-tree-BEE-jo)—Western Settlement.

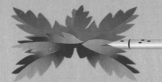
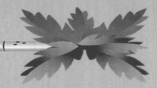

INDEX